A Spirit In Flow

melancholic journey of a random soul

sneha

India | USA | UK

Made with ❤ on the BookLeaf Publishing Platform

www.bookleafpub.in

www.bookleafpub.com

Dedication

I dedicate this book to those who have experienced the universal moment of agonizing pain and confusion and poured them out in the form of verses.

Preface

To me, writing was always an exercise to deal with the things I couldn't share openly with the world. I was fascinated with stories as a child and wanted to be a storyteller for as long as I remember. Every time I sat down to write my thoughts, it came out in the form of verses like an involuntary muscle twitch. Soon, I found myself pouring my heart out in verses and completely surrendering to the thoughts in my mind without filtering or censoring or judgement. It was hard to feel so vulnerable and exposed to myself. Being exposed to my own truth created a vast space inside me for acceptance and change. Now that I am sharing my work with the world, I feel emboldened. This book is an attempt to nudge those who read it to open up a space inside themselves to embrace those parts that we are taught to hide away.

Acknowledgements

My work is a confluence of innumerable encounters I have had with people, places and ideas and their aftermath. I am thankful to the people in my life who have always aroused a sense of curiosity in me to explore my world inside and out.

I thank BookLeaf Publishing and their extensive promotion that left me no choice but to take this bold decision to publish my work. I came across BookLeaf Publishing through social media and listening to their story made me realise that I have no excuses left now to not realise my dreams. I am grateful to the platform for giving me a chance to express myself through my writings.

1. Depth

I am fearless to unravel
Thread by bare thread
Everything that makes me whole

I love the agony of it all
Unbecoming is a sacred ritual
Forging new paths is the goal

Naked and free I roam around
With a lingering gaze that haunts
Gently unmasking every soul

A new height of willful unfolding
I see the truth from a distance
And it only gets sharper up close

I live in a depth untouched
Where demons dance in trance
Where angels sing by chance

2. To make or break

It is a dreadful sight
In the dead of night
Empty streets scream
Not a light in sight

Alone and tired
Of this blinding grief
Where are the hearts
That feel so deep

Waiting for dawn
Blinding or bright
The eyes can see
A flock of birds in flight

So I fly with them
Where could they lead
A new world across the sea
Of infinite possibilities

3. The joy of sadness

Nothing is perhaps more joyous than sadness
It is a baseline that works fine for the times we live in
Chasing unending happiness is a fool's errand
Nothing is more elusive than a fickle paradise
Sadness is a quiet companion who demands nothing
Sadness is the truth that an open mind perceives
I would rather live in an eternal sadness of being
Than seek cheap optimism like a drug addict
My solitude is an ode to sadness that is joyous

Sadness brings no suffering to the soul
As absence of happiness does

4. A sigh of relief

Words fall short to explain
All these mixed emotions accumulated over time
Pounding with the rhythm of my heart they say
'I am here and forever I will stay'

I breathe in heavily longing for relief
Close my eyes and fall into a deeper pit
Clawing and crawling to find some peace
A ray of hope is all I need

Clutching a feeble dream, I arise
Glad to witness another day, another night
I sit beside my emotions and let them be
Until they breathe a sigh of relief and let me be

5. My violent heart

I hear a quiet noise inside
A call not to be ignored
'Listen to me, listen to me'
Take off your blind fold

See for yourself the mess you are
An annoying penchant to grab hold
You want to feel joy and peace
But you cannot handle the oar

Why do you seek the presence of another?
There is no room in your world so cold
What future have you got to offer?
Everything ends in dust as foretold

You think you love too much
You do not care a bit, truth be told
You have no true will to forgo your beliefs
It was all a charade, a story so old

6. The first time I looked at my wound

I went about the world looking for life
In every life, I found profound pain
I saw laughs that cried and cries that laughed
The never ending sorrow that trapped them all

No strong bone could fix a broken heart
No true love could mend a broken mind
No laughter cured the illness begot
No pity pulled up a hand that was lost

I looked down from the summit
The life I sought was nowhere to be found
My broken self, looked up from the abyss
That is when I looked down at my own wound

7. Death in parts

A million times I die
A million times I am reborn
Hit by a passing bullet of words
Or a guillotine that chomps on the heart
Sometimes the rotting chunks were removed by force
The hurt tearing me apart beyond repair
Shattered pieces were dissolved in blood
And returned in new forms to their places
Who was I before and who have I become
A shadow of novelty or a veil of the past
As I search for my form in darkness
A little voice comes forth as a song
A million times I must die yet
And a million times I must be reborn

8. Fire

I am fire
Do not tell me to burn slow
Do not tell me to be mellow
Do not tell me where to go
It is not in my nature to obey commands

I am fire, burning for you, you my wind
Alas, I burn with an overwhelming desire for you
Need I say I begin and end with you, my love, my wind
Either take me in or let me consume everything within

9. Hopeless dawn

It has been long since I woke up feeling happy
No rhyme or reason for this veil of sadness that
Lies heavy on my mind at the first light
The dawn has arrived, but my joy has departed

My heart stays numb in the mornings
Weighed down by hopelessness
Only stony silence for company
No thoughts or ideas, just a stark void

It seems impossible to even smile
Even as the morning sun warms my body
Why are mornings such a hard time?
Where is the morning sunshine of happiness?

Not for me, not for me, not for me

Mornings are a man-made myth
It is nothing but the dying of the night
My nights of solitude that warm the heart
Only to be taken away by the cold dawn

I know, I am a creature of the night.
Who needs morning blues.

10. Existence

I sometimes wonder if I am real
Do I exist when not being witnessed
Who am I if not something to someone
Is it even worth defining a lie

For I only feel love when I give
I find strength when I am needed
I can move mountains for others
But unable to lift a finger for myself

I become a tool to be used
I offer my heart to be abused
I wait to see if I will refuse
To let myself become a muse

I cannot refute the nature of existence
It is not a matter of choice
Nor a helplessness in need of redress
Being really nothing is not a vice

For nothing is a reflection of everything
A mirror for cause and effect
An abyss that absorbs the darkness
A darkness to bring out the light

11. Crying over the grave

I lay dead in the warm ground
Comfortable, quiet and snug
No more laboured breaths to take
No more painful sighs to make
No more fighting the urge to break
No more pondering over mistakes
I see others hovering over my dead body
Some wrought with pain, some with disdain
Some shed a tear or two, some only glare
'Why are they here for a dead body?' I wonder
Is death more amusing than life?
When my body still breathed, was it a bitter sight
If I knew people would rather visit my dead body
Would I grieve their absence while alive
Alas! One never knows what binds souls
Nothing ever lasts in death or life
Everyone leaves muttering incoherent goodbyes
While all I craved for was a pleasant hello when alive

12. Epiphany of life

Holding on to the memory
Closed eyes open a new world
Dreams and reality blur into one lucid emotion
Glimpses of words, familiar yet unknown
Dear to the heart, yet a strange illusion
Constantly running pages of a flipping book
Like the sprinkle of hot-cold showers

Soaking in the feeling
Deep are the valleys of the mind
Twisting and turning with each emotion
Near, yet so far; sweet, yet so sour
Every time the mind touches the deepest thought
Strings of sensation strum a different note
Like a rhapsody of a million musical instruments

Living with presence
Realisation of every connotation
Aware of every emotion and sensation
Real, yet so divine; mundane, yet so alive
Blasting away the black, white and greys
The past and future blend into a million hues
Like an iridescent epiphany of life

13. Fork in the road

When the road seems to end
And there is nowhere left to go
Just stop and look back
There might have been a fork

That uncharted landscape
Still calls you to come forth
Why not take that road?
May be there is still hope

Wandering may not be that bad
Not knowing yet where to go
What lies ahead is a mystery
So many things waiting to unfold

Wondering if it was all a dream
A journey of being lost in the shadow
Therein lies the beauty of life
A goodbye followed by a sweet hello

14. Looking glass

With me, you will find what you want
Seek and you shall receive tenfold
Show me what you hold within
And find yourself without
The possibilities are infinite here
Do not hold back in forethought
Your worst impulses are welcome
Your best intentions are sought
If your truth could lie without blinking
You need not open your mouth
Senses can only get you so far
Deception is the game you bought
Dread not the final conclusion
Even judgements fall short
You think, so you are
You see the core is hot
Fan the flame or tame it
Nonetheless you burn the rot
Win or lose or squander away
I will be here to take it all

Behold the looking glass!

15. Melancholy

Tell me what it is
We are all scared of
Not being seen or
Not being able to hold

Too much is too bad they say
Nothing at all is also not good
How much should it be then
Wish I could learn from you

Is it bravery to live through it all
Is it cowardice to let go
Would anything be worth it at all
To stay calm or let the mind implode

Some will never know
Those who know will make do
And then there are some of us
Who will always stay blue

16. Footsteps

I walk a mile every day
In my shoes and sometimes in others'
The shoes bite here and there
The footsteps become a drill

The path I take leads me on
To corners where the walls stand tall
I try to move on and in my haste
I leave behind rubble and dirt and waste

Miles behind me and miles ahead
My feet are bleeding crimson red
I realise I have been walking on wreckage
Thanking those who walked before me

Each step on rubble and dirt and waste
Is a story of a fool forging a bloody trail
The path has rendered the shoes useless
A wasted attempt at being considerate

Barefoot and wiser the none, I carry on
Leaving the crimson trail behind
I walk across bridges, ravines, taverns and town
In the softness of earth, I begin to revive

I hope the walk takes me to a place
Where days and nights are entwined
No sleep in sight, nor waking hours
Nor sweet release of the aching heart

17. Reverberate

It is cruel, it is true
Apart and blue
Time stands still
When thinking of you
Where it all began
It ended without a clue
Warmth of that embrace
Stuck like glue
Needs and wants
Are long overdue
Rendezvous in solitude
Silence on cue

18. Swing

Life makes us wonder
About things that seem
At once frail and broken
Sometimes a hopeless glee

Not everything is rosy and cozy
Sometimes, it is not what is meant to be
Rocks fall and smash the boulders
Cracking open the wounds that had healed

A sudden splash of cool water
Wakes up the dead strewn feelings
It is a torment to even feel this boundless joy
Like sitting on a swing, once down again high

19. Tilting balance

I screamed at the world today
To terrorise or as a plea to be heard?

I jumped the fence today
To violate or to find an escape?

I poured out my rage today
To harm or an attempt to rid the pain?

I laughed at the absurdity today
To mock or with a shock of dismay?

I cried to my heart's content today
Self-pity or reminiscent of pain?

I fell silent amidst the noise today
Cowardice or deliberate oblivion?

I stood firm against the rising tide today
A foolish rebellion or sweet surrender?

To be aware is a double-edged sword
Acknowledging it cuts deep either way

I cannot bow down to logic and reason
Nor can I die at the altar of emotions

One cannot remain still on a tilting balance

20. Bare necessities

My desires are minute
My goals are simple
My dreams are plain
My hopes are routine

I desire life's minute moments
Where the goal of simply living is enough
With a dream to traverse the plain and rigid
Hoping the routine never gets timid

Because moments bring joy
By simply being lived
A dream in plain sight
Bringing hope to the livid

Yesterday I burned my desires
Threw my goals out the window
My dreams lay shattered
My hopes lost wind

But today I found my moments
Again, I longed to live
My desires, goals, dreams and hopes
Crashed the party all renewed

Oh wretched is tomorrow
Who knows what it brings
Will desires and goals of tomorrow
Kill today's hopes and dreams

I must be lucky to have known
The stuff desires and goals are made of
That dreams work best in the days
And hopes make the nights less cold

21. Who am I?

I am a mystery to myself
I surprise myself a lot
One second I am fuming
The next moment I am soft

I sometimes wonder if
I am playing some game
There are no rules to who I am
Is it necessary to explicitly say it

If today, I am repulsive
Can I not be attractive another day
Is there a design to how I must exist
Is my existence a moral constraint

My flaws are mine alone
Not a reflection of how I am seen
My virtues are mine alone
Ain't nobody in charge of me

I stand alone because I can
Fiercely so when I am at my worst
I am not everyone's cup of strong tea but
The water in me can quench the thirst

The bitterness is just ironic!

22. Belonging

When I sit on a swing
Stand behind me and see me go high
If you want to climb the roof
Let me bring that ladder for you without a sigh

Let me bring you flowers
Get a vase to keep them by your side
You bring the water
Let me fashion a stream for us to slide

For I built everything myself
With a dream of having a life of my own
You found directions in the darkest of times
You walked on your chosen path alone

Walk beside me to a place where we belong
A companion through the valleys and peaks
And if I ever became weary in the end
Bid me farewell and walk on my friend

23. Love and disgust

Why do I do this to myself
Knowing what becomes of me
Every time I come close to you
I dread my desire you see

Can you tell me what this is
A veil between you and I
I cannot see you clearly
Yet I sense a need, but why

Are you in my world waiting
Or am I in yours debating
Is it you or me or is it
A wall of stifling disparity

Every time the fog lifts
I find myself adrift at sea
Not an anchor in sight
I float around mindlessly

Can't you see me clearly
Is my need a trouble you endure
As I crash on a distant shore
I am abandoned from my world and yours

Standing on this distant shore
I see an aversion so discreet
Strong currents crash and fall
But the islands never meet

Besotted heart seeks solace
From this never-ending jitter
How inevitable this separation
I look at the horizon and wonder

24. My ghost

He left without a sound
Not a single warning
His silence rings in my ears
His absence deepens the wound

I hear a distant ruffle
Like someone approaching my door
I check in the hope of finding him there
Alas, it is only a ghost

The haunting is constant
In every corner, every moment
His presence feels so strong
But my eyes never see him around

Does he feel this way too?
Does he run to his door?
Does he feel my absence so strongly?
Am I not even his ghost?

25. An ode to love

Love is easy, to love is easy
Easier said than done
Because love has no definition
It can end as easily as it had begun
Love wounds everyone
Love wounds everyone

Love is warmth in the cold
Love is hope that holds
Love invokes a song so bold
Love removes reasons to fold
Love saves everyone
Love saves everyone

Love can never be sold
Love comes with a price untold
Love compels to cross the threshold
Love dissolves boundaries carved in stone
Love changes everyone
Love changes everyone